PEACHES AND ROSES- EPISODES IN THE NAVAJO DEGRADATION

PEACHES AND ROSES- EPISODES IN THE NAVAJO DEGRADATION

Episoded in the Navajo Degredation

CHARLES TARLTON

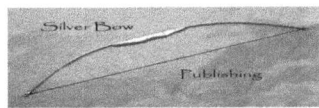

Silver Bow Publishing

CONTENTS

Text Insert	1
Text Insert	2
Text Insert	3
Text Insert	4
Text Insert	5
Text Insert	6
Contents	7
Text Insert	8
Terms For Order	9
Apachu De Nabajo	12
Southwestern Fragment	16
Worst Fears Coming True	21
In The Cycles Of Outrage	24
Westward, Ho! The Navajo!	27
Good To Go	30
Gates Of Irony	33
Dance Around The Fires	37
Peaches And Roses, New Mexico Territory, 1863	41

In The Bright Light Of The Hunt	46
At Fated, Darkened Intersections	49
Manuelito And Kit Carson Argue In The Dawn	52
Violence Embraced	56
The Long Walk To Hweeldi	60
Lost In The Bosque Redondo	64
Return To Dinéta	67
Naabeehó Bináhásdzo (Navajo Nation)	71
Author Profile	79

CARMODY
*We could try imagining the old West right here.
I'll be the Cavalry and you be the Indians.*
BLIGHT
*And while we're imagining things,
we'll let the good guys win this time, right?*

Also by Charles D. Tarlton

Carmody and Blight – The Dialogues
Get Up and Dance
Touching Fire - *New and Selected Ekphrastic Prosimetra*
Fortune's Circle; a Biographical Interpretation of NiccolÁ Machiavelli,

PEACHES AND ROSES:
Episodes in the Navajo Degradation
by
Charles D. Tarlton

Silver Bow Publishing
720 Sixth Street, Unit # 5
New Westminster, BC
CANADA V3L3C5

Title: Peaches and Roses: Episodes in the Navajo Degradation
Author: Charles D. Tarlton
Cover Art: "Desert Illusion" painting by Candice James
Layout and Design: Candice James
Editor: Candice James

All rights reserved including the right to reproduce or translate this book or any portions thereof, in any form without the permission of the publisher. Except for the use of short passages for review purposes, no part of this book may be reproduced, in part or in whole, or transmitted in any form or by any means, electronically or mechanically, including photocopying, recording, or any information or storage retrieval system without prior permission in writing from the publisher or a licence from the Canadian Copyright Collective Agency (Access Copyright).

www.silverbowpublishing.com

info@silverbowpublishing.com

© Silver Bow Publishing 2021

Library and Archives Canada Cataloguing in Publication

Title: Peaches and roses : episodes in the Navajo degradation / by Charles D. Tarlton.
Names: Tarlton, Charles D., 1937- author.
Description: Poems.
Identifiers: Canadiana (print) 20210109254 | Canadiana (ebook) 20210109300 | ISBN 9781774031452 (softcover) | ISBN 9781774031469 (EPUB)
Classification: LCC PS3620.A79 P43 2021 | DDC 811/.6—dc23

Dedication

To all my children:
Rosemary, Jim, Kate, and Sarah Young

Acknowledgements

I would like to thank Megan Arkenberg, one-time editor of *Lacuna: A Journal of Historical Fiction,* who published, in somewhat different form, five of these poems on the Navajos in April 2012, and Clare Macqueen of *Macqueen's Quinterly*, who breathed new life into an old poet.

Contents

CONTENTS

1. Terms for Order, 11
2. *Apachu de Nabajo*, 14
3. Southwestern Fragment, 17
4. Worst Fears Coming True, 21
5. In the Cycles of Outrage, 23
6. Westward, Ho! The Navajo! 26
7. Good to Go, 29
8. Gates of Irony, 32
9. Dance around the Fires, 35
10. Peaches and Roses, 39
11. In the Bright Light of the Hunt, 43
12. At Fated, Darkened Intersections, 46
13. Manuelito and Kit Carson Argue in the Dawn, 48
14. Violence Embraced, 51
15. The Long Walk to Hweeldi, 55
16. Lost in the Bosque Redondo, 58
17. Return to Dinéta, 61
18. *Naabeehó Bináhásdzo* (Navajo Nation), 64

Author Bio ... 71

Terms for Order

1. *The First World was an island, surrounded by oceans, and there lived the first beings who started out in life. Although these beings are referred to as people, they were not people as we know them but were insects and, therefore, they are called the Insect People.* — **Navajo Story of Creation**

From the East
they came walking
over living things.

They dragged
behind them
a driftwood stick

through wet sand
to make a long
line to separate

European humans
from the decimated
trees, wild animals.

From the West
the *Diné* rescuing
lost songbirds,

beg the dying deer's
forgiveness, offer
up life for life.

All the gods arise from stories. What have we here, what grows along the line of shadow from such mountains? Imagine you are unable to see through red rocks or erase the silhouetted pines with the toss of your head. What you can never know you can imagine. The rain falls that lifts the waters up, makes trees and children grow, each season eases into place, its special air and light thrown over us.

The blanket grows in the loom,
the colored sands pour out
in their tight geometrics
softly calling the gods.

Whatever is must have ridden in.
The clearing in front of the hogan
waits. The first
everything, the first
one—first dog, first rock,
first *Hastiin*, first *Asdzan*.

All stories rest in equally precarious balance on the pinnacle of what might be. Stories equally insane—How must all this have happened, how could it?

The MAKER

and the made thing. What we
know. Our maker, then...
Hastseyalti's wild proliferation.

Spontaneous emergence out of the Nothing is only another possibility; some great sleeve pulled inside-out and where hollow vacuums fill it all in, and darkness reveals itself as light, eases into light, is defied by light. I am Coyote, Raven, Eagle, Bear. Animals in me, live in me.

The all-around's
a given. Such unease
as needs account,
imagining something
given, yet unseen.

Explaining something
by nothing, my hand
some godly plan,
the god unknown,
mute, and heard only
in the rattling of
some bright beads.

Apachu de Nabajo

*The Navajos constitute a society in which each individual has a strong sense of belonging with the others who speak the same language and a strong sense of difference and isolation from the rest of humanity. Navajo cohesiveness is due to a common linguistic and cultural heritage, to the occupation of a defined territory and to a common designation for themselves, that is "Dine" or "People," as against all others. They are a distinct land using entity. — **23 Ind. Cl. Comm. 244***

Everywhere in America it was like this. A swell of white European mass rose up, heaved forward, surged against the thin brown line of Indian sand, broke and scattered it. And like the angry sea, could not be contained.

Tumbling backwards,
pebbles, mussel shells,
and polished shards
made only tinkling
noises in the roar of
waves crashing
on the rocks of necessity.

A weight of 40 million Whites against 9,000 Navajos.

The far-reaching, the boundless future will be the era of American greatness. In its magnificent domain of space and time, the nation of many nations is destined to manifest to mankind the excellence of divine principles; to establish on earth the noblest temple ever dedicated to the worship of the Most-

High—the Sacred and the True. Its floor shall be a hemisphere—its roof the firmament of the star-studded heavens.... — **John O'Sullivan**

DISTURBANCES all along the line.

Two forms of life assuming each
their own predestined role
in the rocking of the seasons,
in the unfolding of Time.

Warriors on both sides,
responding in their too glad
moods of violence,
intolerant of challenge, proud
disrespectful of consequences,
preferring the short term
and its immediate gratifications.

    Everything thrown into the balance gave,
    in the longest run, advantages to power.

From the angle of history,
both sides rolled the dice
into the blowing desert wind.
They became synchronous
testaments to our flawed nature.

Two long separate stories
reached out, clawing
for each other around the earth.

I am trying to intrude right here;
the history is all wrapped
around me—I'm neither Navajo

nor a descendant of any
soldier in those hot deserts.

I am struggling with some hard
SYMBOLIC thing,

the echo of the world, faintly
hollowed, wondering when
we will have piled up enough
pain and suffering to reach
our own thin air, the proper
altitude, a lack of substance.

Do I long to breathe
the smoky Hogan air,
sit in the desert sunset,
smell the corncakes,
the wind off the red rocks?

From the East:

Europe's liberated Man

STRUGGLES

—church and empire, popes and kings and parliaments had taken hold of the New World from the one side; and from the West, across the frozen land bridge at Beringia, in an earlier millennium, Outliers from Siberia descended from northern ice into western deserts and carved yellow cities in the stone.

They meet in violent contests up and down the north-south sliding scrimmage line, establishing, irresistibly, the European history in America,

and the PEOPLE's blood flowed.

Creeks and Seminoles, the Kiowa, Comanche, Sioux Cheyenne, Arapaho, Apache, and the Navajo.... herded onto dusty reservations, and their narratives abruptly terminated.

    1.

Southwestern Fragment

At nightfall of this day a Navajo known as Anceluno presented himself in this pueblo soliciting peace in the name of his nation, whose report or message is as follows: that living at Peña Blanca, there arrived at his house a son-in-law of Narbona and another Navajo head-man giving him to understand in the name of ten captains that not finding anyone who would resolve to come as ambassador of the peace of which they treated in a meeting of the major portion of their nation in some dances which they held for that purpose on the other side of de Chelly. — **Jose Andres Sandoval**

In his own voice,
then in my own voice,
as if another offering of trust
had been squandered
under the moon;

and it comes in the bat's eye
night where a gathering
in tumult counseled

under the deceit of a pale waved flag
a messenger of peace

with, perhaps, a cynical smile

HIDDEN

in shadows and a wink,
turning with the dancing,

with the sparkling.

I watch from a distance.
In this, the recognition of what
undercuts even the rose,

the doubling line, the sweetness,
hidden weapons, sharp and protective,
necessary threats. We are eager
to return confidences,
find the long sleepy
night, no disturbances.

The wings take the body up,

the WINGS
envelop the air, thrash in the air
and answer me, give me an answer.

No HESITATION!

There is possibility to reach a settlement, put an end to wanton pleasures
and grave mournings, slow the flow of blood in the cold light.
We count the races and the moon-faced gods.

Slits for eyes, slits
in the stiff drum leather
shields make a thunder
somewhat fainter now
the rain has stopped.

And the wind far off whines over warriors, soft whispering
hidden in slow breaths, in the brush in the dark, when candles are blown out.

The dark cloud came down so
CLOSE.

The spirit of the empty windy street stirred, blew up in dust devils, twisting and darting.

Are there still trees
where the river snaked,
where the zephyrs came
in puffs of pollen, dancing
among the leaves?

Word comes to end war! The word in its initial thrust. The savages have met,
    and they have stood for peace. Dare we believe them?

* * *

They have extensive fields of Corn & Wheat—fine Peach orchards, and grow quantities of Melons, Squashes, Beans and Peas, and have immense flocks of sheep, a great number of Mules and horses of a superior breed. - **James S. Calhoun, "Annual Report of the Commissioner of Indian Affairs," Doc. No. 17. p. 207 (1950).**

It's settled, then, a civilization of sorts.

   . . . [T]hey hold the country over which they roam [by] mere possessory title,
    which the God of nature has permitted them.
Or the god of Nature?

RESEMBLANCES.

And one came on a wind,
on a turquoise wind from the mountain.

He bore a likeness to the cold blood of the joust,
the long singing arrow flies,
the song rises over the top of the shield . . .

Wave after wave
of hungry farmers,
their plows impatient
to cut down and dig up
where the land will
yield its richness. Wealth
was proven in the stacks
of hay, the cribs of corn,
bushels of sweet

PEACHES.

A dream of juice,
the clink of golden coins
down the chins,
of fresh bread from an oven
in the shade
of the canyon walls.

They can grow anything around here.

    They came ready to tear open the land; a desperation born of disaffection
    readied by despoiling. The wilderness put under the plow where already
    there was the perfect form of life—

IINÁ.

There was little difference
between what the land offered,

and what the people needed.

Worst Fears Coming True

> *In particular, a succession of comets that came raining down on the Earth in the year 1833 were interpreted by many Navajo as a sign of bad times to come. This event was followed by an increasing crescendo of warfare among the Navajo's neighbors - a period known as Naahoondzood ["Time of Fear"].*
> — **Neal W. Ackerly**

A fattened geometry of tears
and shed blood comes into the line:
we might call it— working

KNOWLEDGE.

The same taut membranes
as when angels hammer harp strings,
sympathetic harmonies surrounding,
like dogs around a tail in heat.

As when, from two days
in the saddle, in unclean
underwear, the skin breaks
into sores and bleeding rashes,
and guilt hangs like a distant
thunderstorm on the desert,
black and heavy and slow.

The truth of the world did not just recently go sour. We did not discover doubt for the first time today, like some abandoned infant under the porch light.

Uncertainty has clamored, a constant beating on the door. The terrible mumblings inside,
the wide-eyed terrors outside, shouted it, but we always held it off.

Is all it is, verses rising
in the absence of gravity
light verses on the wind.

The desert night carries the old voices far and for a long time. The heat of the desert
scalds dry flakes off everyone's skin, face and forearms grow dark and black, leathery.

War was born just so!
In the eyeless distances,
the hot air flattened
against skin.

Desert peoples are like that, long dead things on the surface, on their hides;
eyes flat and watered down, diluted and dried out by the hot light.

And what I know of deserts
—too much light, too dry.
Hot air comes to you
as from an opened oven,
weird plants and horned toads,
noisy snakes and buzzards.

The rivers are but
memories of rivers,
sand and rocks, high

on the mountains, purple
in the twilight, no tree grows.

In the Cycles of Outrage

I have been a Captain ever since I was a young man. I have come to tell my Great Father that my people wish to live in peace & quiet. I have lost my grandfather and two other members of my family who were all killed by Mexicans. I have never sought revenge -- My hair is beginning to get gray -- I wish to live in peace with everyone -- I want to see my cattle and horses to be well grazed and my sheep to be safely herded -- and to get fat -- which can never be done while my people are at war. Is it American justice that we must give up everything and receive nothing? **—Chief Armijo at the Council of Jemez Springs (1852)**

Caught

in a HOT

dry twister on flat ground; nowhere to hide. Surrounded by contrary wills frustrating every gesture; sometimes with a reason, often just for the chance they are beyond reach. They are deaf and dumb to

ME.

It is an old story, this feuding. When it started is always vague, forgotten.
That way, every depredation is retaliation; there is always the other to blame.
We are only striking

BACK.

It is hugely pleasant
to go on a wild raid,
to dress up, paint up,
ride through the night,
strike before attesting dawn.
Kill the careless,
drive away the horses and sheep,
carry off a woman or two,
a child for a slave.
But get back home before they come for *their* revenge.

Scouts on the high rocks.
A fire a torch is waved
a whistle, a shout
and the women round up
everyone, and herd the children
into a safe arroyo
holding the horses' noses,
shushing the babies.

Staging it all to end the

DREAM of peace;

they talk and dance into the morning hours. There were a thousand treaties, broken as soon as they were signed. "You do *not* speak for me!"

Everyone agrees on terms,
unfair perhaps, but better
than no terms at all.
Then, as it turns out,
someone was not there to sign,
or had no right to sign, or signed
with a deceitful heart.

And just as you set down
to a long-awaited sleep,
Utes, Apaches, Mexicans
or New Mexicans,
Apachu de Nabajo thundered
through the village.

I am so TIRED of war.
Will we ever have enough to eat,
or time enough for talk and love?

Like yeast stirred into batter,
the wild ones cannot wait.

They RISE up!

They dream only of adventure, risk, the easy way.
Their heads are filled with heroic stories,
and big talk of hatred and the enemy.

They see no distance,
they hear nothing from far off,
they lie down in their beds
only till they can get up again.

Impatience is no strategy
against a large, ambitious,
a will roaring sea.

Westward, Ho! The Navajo!

[T]he policy pursued toward the Indians has resulted favorably...many tribes of Indians have been induced to settle upon reservations, to cultivate the soil, to perform productive labor of various kinds, and to partially accept them to avoid extermination. **U.S. Grant**

And monstrous murder narrowly eludes the otherwise blind push into these few islands of submission where the defeated whimper in their chains.

That unsaid....

WELL, OF COURSE!

Dreams of gold and silver under hunting grounds, best grazing for cattle, and it turns out
    all was exactly where the *Diné* herded horses and sheep.

We Americans, pretending we'd found

FORGOTTEN or LOST

money in the street or were only entering

ABANDONED

houses, taking it for granted we could

STEAL

whatever we found.

ALREADY

encamped Indians were in the way. Brute force was all to them and nothing else.

Imagine that, instead of Navajo, they had found settled there before we came Frederick's   Prussian *Deutsches Heer* or armed Samurai, *Gempeitōkitsu* (????),
pre-eminent in the Arts, both swords and poetry.

We would have had to restrain our famous Destiny (and it would then have seemed far less Manifest) somewhere nearer Newton, Mass. or Ramapo, N.J.

TURNABOUT

Like Cyclops, we ingested them,
the national peristalsis defecating the result
in our own image out the back
of our machine for devouring the continent.

Those we didn't kill, we forgot.
They had learned to dress up in wool,
talk like Hoosiers or Virginians;

many went to school in Pennsylvania
learning to be White.
You find their sad burlesques
in photo albums now,
lost young Navajo men
in trousers and boots,
staring into the camera,

their soft wild eyes
like the eyes of a trapped animal.

EXTERMINATE.

To be exact, the term was used
to threaten just what consequences
native armed resistances would excite.

The other cold ironic word
that burns so fiery now
up from the pages of the Army's
frontier correspondence

is (Oh, no! Oh, no!)

CONCENTRATION!

in referring to planned
involuntary reservations,
especially the Bosque Redondo,
where the Navajos were herded up
and made to go.

Good to Go

For a long time past the Navajoe [sic] Indians have murdered and robbed the people of New Mexico. Last winter when eighteen of their chiefs came to Santa Fe to have a talk, they were warned, and were told to inform their people, that for these murders and robberies the tribe must be punished, unless some binding guarantees should be given that in future these outrages should cease — **Brigadier General James H. Carleton***

I would remark that the Navajoes [sic] everywhere evinced the most earnest desire for peace. I am not prepared to say what would be the better line of policy towards them, but there is no doubt that a war made upon them now by us would fall the heaviest upon the least guilty, would transform a nation which has already made considerable progress in civilized arts into a race of beggars, vagabonds and robbers. — **Capt. John G. Walker**

A long ancestral legacy running back from you and me, along our fathers and their fathers' fathers' lines, lost and unremembered, stood poised to strike them, strike the Indians, in this case, Navajos.

An IRRITANT,

and us impatient for the striking, lightning and the darting jab of Rattlesnake;
Quickly now, history is waiting!

When you step into the yaw of time,
step in there gingerly
or it might swallow us alive, lay up a curse:

a curse might not be worked
to full horror for a century or more.

We ought to have learned, from our cold tormenting of the Navajos:
you never cut down a man's olive trees; the gods become too furious.

And we ignore the devils,
wood sprites, and calling birds
chattering in the last seconds
of the dark. A deliberate deformity
in the evolution of the world
and at some peril: broken savages.

They are patient
when we are not, methodical
when we rush blindly forth.
Call back along the line of history,

go more slowly.

We've never known the fullest
consequence, of such

WILDNESS.

Eager, greedy, festering,
actions in a fit—
tormenting, starving out,
belittling, torturing some,

and then, oh, the evil gets so easy,
roles fit more comfortably,
whoever is an obstacle,
the slightest annoyance . . .

A man of peace, a man of war
wrestling on the desert floor.

In morally as well as other ways
it will be costly this exterminating.

But when the time came, and they had scoured down the Navajo in a savage war, they said,

ATTRITION,

as if it were a euphemism. They cleaned out the nest and rolled the eggs along in the sand, kicking them (as we will find) and shooting stragglers.

Guilt in war? We hesitate, a hundred-sixty years ago; so many books and films have numbed our sensitivity to murder and revenge.

The only good Indian....Then, they were no more. There were no more

Diné
Peaches
Hogans
Roses
Navajos

in the Canyon de Chelly.

        * U.S. Cavalry leader on the Navajo's "long walk"
        to Bosque Redondo.

Gates of Irony

Cage the badger and he will try to break from his prison and regain his native hole. Chain the eagle to the ground - he will strive to gain his freedom, and though he fails, he will lift his head and look up at the sky which is home - and we want to return to our mountains and plains, where we used to plant corn, wheat and beans. — **A Navajo in 1865.**

The timber wolves
in the National Zoo,
behind hardened
endless chain link fences
pace in the unsettled dust underfoot,
their ice-gray eyes
restless in captivity,
focusing black irises
on their long walk to nowhere,
endlessly, tirelessly searching.

Something of the poetic art,
in which dead Navajo texts
breathe on me here
in the still unsettled dust
of their captivity,
on the long walk to nowhere.

Ice-gray eyes: hard, dark
apertures in black iris
diaphragms, the Wolf's.

See how, along the way, society constrains us, holds our desires down, displaces pleasure with its stern commands, requires that we

WORK

for the broken weld,
untwisted wire,
the shadow falls just so
across the soldiered joint,
and where the exactly,
the unexpected would spell

FREEDOM,
freedom, "freedom," *da'ahiniita*

Natural ways, like manners more direct and wet, scratching in the dirt those primitive vocables, and a hurried breath when it's suppressed, boils in us, turns ineffectually inward and inflicts distress neurotically.

I can read the corn,
calculate sandy desert
distances along the wind
by dust clouds
and the smell of the river.

Multiplication tables
and a white shirt,
dinner at a formal table,
sitting up on chairs.

Makes you think twice.

What of my own interiority
that struggles here
against imaginary chains,

resents fences and barriers,
that makes me want to howl

—like the WOLF?

We recognize the nakedness with which we Europeans, a thousand miles into the wilderness, took our frustrations out on Indians as targets we defined

OUTSIDE

the boundaries of our moral codes.

ANIMALS,

perhaps, but not human strictly speaking, they might be freely dealt with kicked, brushed aside, or killed in the streets.

A stilted and political rhetoric allowed our actions to be staged; small, pitifully self-congratulatory, unquestioningly pushed by a will to inflict.

Before imaginary scenery,
acting out with our eyes closed
fictions that assuage
our consciences. Consider:

When marauding regional
militias form up to raid
quiet Navajo villages
where women and children sleep,

a prayer or two and everyone
feels they're acting in the name
of the Garden, part of something holy,

and

INEVITABLE.

Dance Around the Fires

Aside from all considerations of humanity the extermination [!] of such a people will be the work of the greatest difficulty. **—Lt. Colonel Edward R. S. Canby, U.S.A.**

We'll first chastise, then civilize, bold Johnny Navajo. **—Santa Fe Gazette, December 8, 1863**

Hot winds stirred up by a thousand-thousand horses blow leaves brightly dead yellow and red under the desert sky's hard dome, blow up in close clouds, billowed in front of distant mountains, some stick against a stone, some collected in the damp pools of a creek bed—dead leaves.

It is a cold wind
can play
a killing song
so sweetly,
without rancor.

IT IS SOME WAR!

Or the wind itself
blows on the leaves,
the dead red leaves,
and fluttering, jiggles
the sweet yellow peaches
swinging on leafy stems:

and the leaves sing

a leaf's song,
call the wind master or slave.

In the canyon of harnessed winds and leaves
in the one hollow of red stones and the river,
time rubs and opens its eyes.
In the first contacts,

an INTRUSION

added, aggravations, hunger, a tightening of distances.

How to get beneath the skin to listen to blood and read the soft drum tapping, to scatter barriers when barriers are being built eye-view: confident in the whip, the size and snaky heft of it in the longest run.

A continent and an endless flood of

Men
Wagons
Guns
Flour
Beer

A bravery seldom tested either way, but face to face.

On his knees
in a New Hampshire furrow
weeding around the precious
corn shoots, a boy dreamed
of a wild ride on an Indian pony
across the sparse grass
of the prairies, somewhere

he GUESSED

in Nebraska or Wyoming,
the Arapahos, Sioux, Cheyenne
yelping behind him;
he turned, let off a shout his own
and felt his heart pound.

"EEEYYYIIIEEE!!!!"

Strangers, they have come
to the edge of their own world,
to the beginning
of unexpected creatures,
unheard of geography,
on the horizon
a low-lying line of mountains.

Soldiers,
fresh from their own fratricide,
and posted to the moon.

    INTERLUDE: "Manuelito* Speaks" (the Movie)

FADE IN:

INT. NAVAJO HOGAN – A GATHERING OF WARRIORS – NIGHT

                MANUELITO
      They come here speaking of oceans,
      of water-walking for days, floating on
      the water in human waves, pilling up,
   pushing in here from a world of machines.

      Their big guns, they live where the big

guns grow. They make the sky burn.
They eat one another. They sleep in the
ground. They have come to master the *Diné*.

COYOTE
An urge to dance comes over you, the dust
on your moccasins, your boots, with the sun
slipping behind the red-tipped hills, the fire
of the dance, the lifting, the falling, the rolling
over and around.

CHOREOGRAPHER
What do we realize in their dancing? What do
we learn of men suddenly free'd in the wilderness,
cut loose. Who EXACTLY were the savages?

---

* Leader of the Navajo, first in resistance and then on the "long walk" to Bosque Redondo. Like many Navajo, Manuelito was was known by other names depending upon context. He was *Ashkii Diyinii* (Holy Boy), *Dahaana Baadaané* (Son-in-Law of Late Texan), *Hastiin Ch'ilhaajinii* ("Man of the Black Plants Place") and as *Nabááh Jiłt'aa* (War Chief, "Warrior Grabbed Enemy") to other Diné.

Peaches and Roses, New Mexico Territory, 1863

On the 3d Moved Camp about 3 miles no. [to] another Orchard. there I cut down 500 of the best Peach trees I have ever seen in the Country, every one of them bearing Fruit. — **Captain John Thompson**

Found in our camp a rather rare thing in this country, abundance of wild rose bushes. Gathered and prepared some sprigs for home on the Hudson. — **Captain Eben Everett**

It was the thorn that plotted to outsmart
The cunning of the rose. — **Henri Coulette**

Shaken to the ground, rare, sweet desert peaches scattered each time the black axes cut through the smooth hard skin to the soft heartwood underneath. The trees would shudder and sigh as they rolled over on their green crowns and thrust branches out in front to break an awkward fall.

Lowing cattle,
reluctant in the chute,
wait to be stunned;
you can hear the captive bolt,
but they all bleed to death.

The real horror
lies in the magnitude
of our misdeeds,
in the difference

between a murder
and a massacre.

All day, into the night, they hauled in the ragged downed trees. You could hear the ring and rattle of the horses' collars, the slap of the traces, the horses snorting as they came out of the dark and into the fire's circle. The soldiers stacked uprooted peach-tree mountains and set them alight. In the hot smoke, the smell of fruit roughly cooking, sweet then bitter, a harsh syrup in the air.

Just a job of work;
they might have been hauling
oak beer barrels
in a bustling city street,
up into the pub.

All the orange trees
in southern California
were bulldozed out
and stacked in huge jumbles
to make way for stucco houses.
They burned all through the night.

The *auto-da-fé* of Navajo peach trees threw shadows against the canyon's red-rock walls, making twisting silhouettes of the laboring soldiers' dance. In twos and threes, they stooped and hauled, turned and pulled, a slow gigantic Death-ballet in the twisting light.

The symbolism
of bonfires is not lost.
Around the world
they burn in hot vengeance
or wild celebration.

Wayang shadow dancers

tell the story
of the bloody battle of *Kurukshetra*,
a mythology for war

A ghoulish military operation, this hunting down and destruction of peaches, was executed without sentiment. Mounted soldiers searched the length of the Canyon de Chelly, and on the way they found and tore up planted melons and squash, ripped out the beans, and stole the corn for their horses.

It is prohibited to attack, destroy, remove, or render useless objects indispensable to the survival of the civilian population, such as foodstuffs, agricultural areas for the production of foodstuffs, crops, livestock, drinking water installations and supplies, and irrigation works, for the specific purpose of denying them for their sustenance value to the civilian population or to the adverse Party, whatever the motive, whether in order to starve out civilians, to cause them to move away, or for any other motive.— **The Geneva Conventions**

Vietnam-war
veterans came home
having destroyed
whole towns and villages,
remembering dead friends.

My uncle George Molstad
recalled how, on the way back
from bombing raids on Germany,
all the guns on his B-17
strafed every living thing.

Searching later for ripe peach trees they might have missed the first time, another Captain of Horse from New York came upon thorny wild roses cast among the stones.

Back in the church,
where thirty years before
I had served mass,
the same long late shadows,
redolence of chancel flowers.

A rainy spell
and purple wildflowers
coming down the Grapevine
rise from the desert floor.
Oh, you had to be there!

In 1898 Prof. E. O. Wooton described a remarkable new rose from southern New Mexico, giving it the name Rosa stellata on account of the stellate trichomes. The peculiar, mostly trifoliolate leaves, the leaflets with cuneiform bases and more or less truncate, sharply toothed apices, gave the plant an unusual appearance; while even the flowers, described as large and showy, deep rose-purple, were not at all like those of the ordinary wild roses of the Rocky Mountains — T. D. A. Cockerell (1913)

How much do the prickly desert rose sprigs weigh when we carry them home to grow along a fence in Coxsacki or Schodack Landing, where a wife might wait and watch every day for the Mary Powell steaming up against the current and the tide from Beacon or Catskill on her way to Albany?

On the tarmac
at Auckland airport, 1972,
they sprayed the plane
with insecticide—
up and down the aisle.

Steady prairie winds,
blowing the transgenic corn
onto pure organic fields,
forget dwarf thoroughbreds,

maximizing the yield

The fires burned out and settled down to peach coals; the Captain's roses, wrapped in coarse dampened cloth rested in a rolled slicker.

The peaches, small, hard,
red-yellow clingstones
were used mostly dried.
They had come from China,
brought by Conquistadores.

In the Bright Light of the Hunt

An Indian is a more watchful and a more wary animal than a deer. He must be hunted with skill he cannot be blundered upon; nor will he allow his pursuers to come upon him when he knows it, unless he's the stronger. — **Major General James Henry Carleton**

We have shown the Indians that in no place, however formidable or inaccessible in their opinion, are they safe from the pursuit of the troops of this command; and have convinced a large portion of them that the struggle on their part is a hopeless one. — **Christopher "Kit" Carson***

Out here, from any escarpment, you can see rainstorms from fifty miles away moving slowly, lightning dropping underneath them, lending a better sense of scale.

The plan, to drive the Navajo ahead of us; the army, to push them off their rancherias,

While they hide in the
mesquite and scrub pine,
we'll trample the corn,
burn the houses,
pollute the water,
break up the pottery,
and empty stores
on the hungry ground.

Cornered in the Canyon de Chelly!

My brothers! Brothers!
(high in the shadows
a wild shaman
withers the alien soldiers
with a painted look)!

SING of the rocks!

No one might come
upon you and ignore
your raw nobility.

Lords of the Earth
demanding
to be heard,
to be listened to.

Snakes, tumble weed,
and the bark scorpion,

its STINGER hanging

over us, like the shadow
of a monstrance.

Sing, race in the wind! Sing in the hypnotic chanting, warnings of fierce gods from underworlds unknown,

North wind rises
on the stone face,
blows through cracks
like reeds, a music twirling
in the dusty cathedral of red rock,

rises to heaven,
and looks coolly down

From a childhood of reading Indian adventures, this: the WOLF moved silently without effort, but with purpose.

Careful as thread and whisper sculpting of the slightest turning of a twig, a leaf, a stone, on the hunt, they moved in quiet, seeing, hearing, and smelling everything. Their eyes fastened on the prey. Ears throw out the widest loops, their noses twist and twitch in a bath of WILD scents.

In an art
of rare communing,
dissolve the crystals
of your self
in the heat,
in the cool moonlight,
under the eyes
of your pursuer,
in the path
of the bullet
fastened to fate.

I wondered, then, if what ran in me, in the rivers of my reveries, could reach into the desert, could find the crystal nucleus and make it grow into black, blue, yellow, white glass palaces unreachable, invulnerable,

and SAFE.

*19th century American thug and political assassin. Helped force the Navajo on to Bosque Redondo.

At Fated, Darkened Intersections

And so, with no one to fight, Carson's campaign became, of necessity, a war of grinding attrition. . . He threw himself into this dark work. — **Hampton Sides**

When the Americans first came, we had a big dance, and they danced with our women. We also traded. — **Manuelito**

Answer his most pressing question, represent his deepest fears, the most recurrent ones ("recurrent" from the Latin "run or hasten")

BACK,

return and again stand forth, pause, draw fear unblinking from Antelope's eyes into the stone, high on unlit cavern ceilings, carve (as Carson's soldiers carved their Kilroys on the pink and orange cathedral walls of Canyon de Chelly) your own and everyone's

TRUTHS.

In my head, between long dead Indians and soldiers, there's a world of difference.

The ways they lived,
costumes and food.
How they would answer

WHY?

Given white flour and whole raw coffee beans to tide them over, Navajos in Bosque Redondo simply mixed them both up with water, boiled to make a stew and got deathly sick.

Some fell behind on the long walk in the desert. The column stretched for miles, some fell behind, and the soldiers dropped back to shoot them, they fell behind like crippled horses.

The figuration of our PROGRESS.

Sing out! Sing out! You pious choirs in Springfield and Pittsburg.

Worn down
from wrestling

at the CONFLUENCE of races,

Red and White,
traffic stalls, the blows come
more heavily, slower,
but do more damage.

How can we even talk this way?

A literacy of violence, sharpened up,
cuts through the perfect tense,
in an arc of the passive voice,
uttered in breathless subjunctives—

it all might have been done so DIFFERENTLY.

The colonel's heart a murderer's, at heart
his order bleak, stark, and bloody,

brooking no reluctance,
sent trembling through the ranks.

Manuelito and Kit Carson Argue in the Dawn

The whites were always trying to make the Indians give up their life and live like white men – go to farming, work hard and do as they did – and the Indians did not know how to do that, and did not want to anyway... If the Indians had tried to make the whites live like them, the whites would have resisted, and it was the same way with many Indians. — **Manuelito**

They'll all soon be gone, anyhow. — **Kit Carson**

You were always meant to carry something back with you, something you'd picked up on your vision quest. You looked hard to see how water twisted around the rocks in the stream, that rocks dissolved in tactile evidence, that water that danced its mirroring reflections, how it gathered everything, bent it in quicksilver, and made it dance. That one might talk (one's will the only obstacle).

> With the stones,
> overhear the deepest
> truths the water
> tells the sky's reflections
> once it had captured
> them in its twisting,
> cooling movements.

A long poor life or a short one, the prisoner learned the meanings in the walls by heart, learned to love the close fit, the dust, the peeling paint.

Here's an Indian, an idea in itself, and there a White self, thin as cellophane; you see right through.

Stretching out along a long thin road in the desert you can see the old trailers and upended, dead refrigerators, bent sheets of corrugated steel (from torn-up roofs) where once a race of warriors rode on fearsome ponies and wild, their ideas storming into the hearts of their enemies.

CONJURING enemies . . .

They came in droves,
smacking their lips.

I want, entirely, to listen.

Scattering, the sand in the wind,
pelting in rat-a-tat
the roof of the gas station,
where only one pump is working,
and a beer can rolls along,
also in the wind,
and the sun reluctantly
goes down, goes slowly down
erasing the ugliness.

Distantly, red rocks glow,
needles, towers and elephants
of rocks kick the last orange bits
of the day into the air
one last time, over the shacks.

More abstractly than imagined,
the deal was struck. An exchange
of circumstance, switched cultures.
Here we cut off the flow of artifacts,

sustain the one — Trade in
my wandering across the land,
for milled flour and sugar,
swap game for packaged foods,
give up mesquite fires at night,
tending corn and peaches,
the herds of sheep, the occasional

RAID,

and now, in exchange,
an old pickup, wasting diseases,
loan sharks, teenage suicide,
diabetes, cervical cancer,
tuberculosis, black mold,
but still, dirt floors.

A pride silhouetted, thin, a ricochet.

They might otherwise have been warriors, stumble out of the bar, into the night. The roar of a semi blows through the settlement, the smell of diesel, burned rubber. The red taillights shrink in the distance, the hole filled in with quiet.

The last restless soul
turns in the bed one more time
and falls asleep.
The darkness
waits now by itself
for the dawn, for the sun
to illuminate
in one blinding
unseen second

The red rocks of *Dinétah*.

Each morning, before anything stirs, the world is red in the sun's first light, the world is, for this second, old and pure.

The GHOSTS

of Manuelito and Kit Carson are heard arguing in the red canyons, in the borrowed voices of hurrying coyotes.

Violence Embraced

But these white men...they do not even care. They kill whom they please. They are arrogant and untrustworthy. I want nothing more of their bargains. — **Manuelito**

[T]here is now no choice between their absolute extermination or their removal and colonization at points so remote... as to isolate them entirely from the inhabitants of the Territory. — **Lt. Colonel Edward R. S. Canby.**

They go back to the innocent consciousness of a wild beast of prey, as joyful monsters, who perhaps walk away from a dreadful sequence of murder, arson, rape, and torture with an exhilaration and spiritual equilibrium. — **Nietzsche**

No already patterned history
no established narrative,

no violence or poetry can
define the place
where we now position current efforts.

Violent acts today or poetic ones
begin always fresh, as from

the START

Everyone works with the materials at hand.

Two blindfolded victims,

alternating agents
armed with long bare sticks
swung in widening arcs.

The wind, the sounds
catch each other with a clash,
poised for a second,
then slide off
into a longer,
slower curve around.

One high, one low,
a *ballet d'action*
of whispering blows,
unheard rhythms leaping
unknown melodies.

The lines we were drawing between the species, working subtly (we required) policies as shameful as....

Obedience decided
under the gun;
a clamoring outside.
How in no little distance
I can see and hear
rattling of readied
ploughs, the cough
and stamp of draught
horses, children crying
and then shushed, waiting.

CANNONS ROAR, THE TRAIN'S STEAM WHISTLE

—Land rush! Land grab!

In an emptiness, unseen, a dark quick shadow on a rock, a rustle of sagebrush, the disbelieving eyes of the *Diné*, believing the land, animals and clouds, the wind, the river, canyon walls, the whisper of Owl, the howl of Coyote are all the same with themselves.

    A regiment of cavalry,
    and the wagons hitched,
    stretching in a line
    with oxen and mules,
    impatient, blinded,
    hungry settlers entering

an EMPTINESS,

some frontier,

ALREADY OCCUPIED! INHABITED!

    A broom of cannon
    to sweep away
    all that was in the way.

The flick of a sharp officer's quirt, the wave of a chief's magic feather quickly in and quickly out, a war cry, and a long, loud laugh; some tradition of warfare—little more than a game

AGAINST

    the slow, thick, heavy thud
    of a couple of companies of dragoons,
    the rolling howitzers, war horses,
    the blowing wall of smoke and fire,

    air thicker with bullets than arrows.

Parry and thrust
against the dull
weight of a tide.

Navajos could slip a punch, however,
hit and run, and fade into the night,
leaving virtually no trace.

Infuriating!

O, VIET CONG! O, TALIBAN!

"Stand still and fight!" the elephant roars; the heavier torso of the whole people.

During this year Kit Carson invaded the Navajo country, killed the sheep, burned the cornfields, and took possession of water holes, thereby forcing the surrender of the whole tribe. The number of prisoners held at Bosque Redondo was 7,300 which was believed to include the whole tribe and doubtless was 90 per cent of all the Navajos in New Mexico and Arizona. — **Herbert E. Gregory**

Women, children, elderly,
the crops, the flocks, submit,
but we need chains
to hold the warriors down.

The Long Walk to Hweeldi

The purpose now is never to relax the application of force with a people that can no more be trusted than you can trust the wolves that run through their mountains; to gather them together, little by little, on to a reservation, away from their haunts and hills, and hiding places of their country; and then to be kind to them; there teach their children how to read and write; teach them the arts of peace; teach them the truths of Christianity. — **Brigadier General James H. Carleton**

The tired and ragged people struggled to get to Fort Sumner. Coyotes began to follow the Navajos and crows circled over their heads. They were waiting for somebody to die. The line of weary prisoners became so long the Army could not protect all the people from enemy attacks. New Mexican raiders attacked the Navajos and took their children. . . Many people were stoned to death by revenge seekers while young women and children were captured for slave trade. — **Adam J. Teller**

Wildness that cannot be overcome, can be (the spirit broken and the stubborn mind made docile) flattened under great pressure.

The mustang,
in full liberty of mountains,
runs along the wind,
as if freedom were
only a habit unwisely formed,
carelessly slighting
rules always known,
a looseness of character,
lack of firmness in the frame.

As the Panthera's pride
cringes under the caged whip
and backs away
frightened of a chair!

Navajo Lords of the Earth
brought around, an entertainment
for children, the butt of the clown's
crude gestures, his vulgar painted flair.

Your noble savage
will accept the regimen
of toilette, straighten up his tie,
wear stiff shoes,
and oil his hair, eventually.

We will lead him to the one true God.

Look! Behind the tree! Did you see him?

COYOTE!

They that once ran the pack,
thrusted their hands
in the spilled blood,
they will forget it
in sweet intonations,
clean white cloths of the church;
they will learn to sing
honeyed melodies,
keep their slow rhythms,
follow the baton,
know words of our eternal praise.

They will now eat with a fork,
wash their socks, be like us.

REHABILITATION—such a lasting word!

So many uses,
covering unrolled bolts,
flat acres of delusion,
and casual cruelty.

A higher motive cleansing the cuts
and blows, the roar of cannons.

No angle odd enough, the urging along, the faint cracking of whips, impatient scolding, hands thrown in the air. 'They, none of them, speak English,' a lieutenant moans.

(They speak plenty good
straight talk, this stick!)

Cold dust in our eyes rises up
from scatterings of snow,
the blood hard and muddy
on torn moccasins.
A cloud all around.
Endless up ahead,
behind, a river of *Diné*!
A herd of *Diné*! A storm cloud,
the wide sea dunes, drifts,
floods of *Diné*.
Mist-wolves dog our trail,
a smoke of *Diné* blown,
stretching across passing canyons.

We are the dream soldiers,

their waking and sleeping
become our polestars,
tracking a way, forlorn, unfamiliar,
unwritten, into an arid
and shameful desert.

Lost in the Bosque Redondo

I beg respectfully to call the serious attention of the government to the destitute condition of the captives, and beg for the authority to provide clothing for the women and children. But whatever is to be done should be done at once. At all events... we can feed them cheaper than we can fight them. — **Brigadier General James H. Carleton (Report on the Condition of the Tribes)**

Probably no folk has ever had a greater shock. Proud, they saw their properties destroyed and knew what it was to be dependent upon the largess of strangers. Not understanding group captivity and accustomed to move freely over great spaces, they knew the misery of confinement with a limited area. Taken far from the rugged and vivid landscape which they prized so highly, they lived in a flat and colorless region, eating alien foods and drinking bitter water which make them ill. — **Clyde Kluckholm**

An historical fragrance, an odor of poetry along angles of sunlight at five. The appetite for story. Birds in cages, wild birds, with their wings tied down, kept back from the wire bars, limp and passive, fatalist birds singing a slow song.

Where a Navajo lives
in a dirt hole,
rolls in the dust and dung,
leans into the plow
with total distraction,
a numb hatred,
fear of flogging,

life at hard labor,
falls onto his shoulder.

The long light at five,
raises in his throat a sourness;
his wife waits in the ration line
for the useless tubs, cups, pans
the indigestible victuals;
and a hard, cold night falls
on the Navajo, caged up
all along the Pecos.

Article 5: Any Indian who shall wantonly destroy any trees or farm produce on the reservation shall be confined at hard labor. — **Bosque Redondo Code**

We respond to the golden rule,
too lately made,
with manacles and hoes.

Altsoba "all-war girl"
and *Doba* "no-war girl"
toss roughly in their sleep
and dream of peaches burning,
smell cooking fruit,
hear the loud soldiers talk and laugh.

Make them plant cottonwoods along the moist banks of the alkaline river, stick the shoots right into the mud.

A General's FANTASY

of shade and dreamy punts and parasols along a magical river; quiet cool drifting Navajo children singing. All people that on earth do dwell.

Walking home from Sunday school in billowing skirts and blackened boots. Wakened from cold reverie, their mothers under the mud-covered huts thrown up over the dug holes in rows, a fire of little sticks —their exceedingly simple culinary operations leave little to chance. Nor imagine the reach of plans and calculations.

Even as distant as the nearest horizon, where events (warriors on warhorses, empty water barrels, saline wells and spring) conjure an illogical enemy who will not take the bait.

Roll in, then, like waves of a sudden on the beach where a recent dune erodes, like the fall of a ploughed furrow made in shells and stones that were here long before the slightest liftings off the sea floor, where the wind, unseen, pushes dire events your way.

As events arise before. . .and unforeseen.

Insects invade the corn and the squash perish in aridity. Venereal diseases race from soldiers to captive children and back.

The jaws of Providence

CLOSE

Return to Dinéta

ARTICLE 13. The tribe herein named, by their representatives, parties to this treaty, agree to make the reservation herein described their permanent home, and they will not as a tribe make any permanent settlement elsewhere. . . that they will do all they can to induce Indians now away from reservation set apart for the exclusive use and occupation of the Indians, leading a nomadic life, or engaged in war against the people of the United States, to abandon such a life and settle permanently in one of the territorial reservations set apart for the exclusive use and occupation of the Indians. — **Treaty of 1868**

It was called the "long walk home". A line of about 7,000 Navajos stretched for approximately ten miles. They were leaving Bosque Redondo. It was June 1868. Navajos were coming home. Days of walking were rewarded. Their sacred Blue Bead Mountain came into view. Navajos broke into tears at the welcoming sight. . . When they saw that mountain, the peaks, people cried because, you know, they were coming close to their homeland. — **Peter Iverson**

Coyote running wildly in circles, trying to spit out the rocks in his mouth; he was not used to being cornered. He ran here, he ran there, Coyote wanted to run free. The *Diné* all around him in a ring; they stepped back, a way parted, and Coyote ran through, heading East.

—Home! Home! the People cheered!

What are the limits of paradox? The longest circle?

In order to ensure the civilization of the Indians entering into this treaty. . . a teacher competent to teach the elementary branches of an English education shall be furnished, who will reside among said Indians. — **The Treaty**

The wider the boundary conjured from within the wilder life of the Indians, the larger the reservation necessary to learn the pastoral life and gain dependable subsistence,

and ABANDONING

precarious supplies to be derived
from the chase.

A living mass, the line stretched out ten miles.
Perspective's arrow
aimed for Diné Bikéyah
in the held breaths,
an inward dancing.

The Navajo are not wild! In the tones of practicality, liberation is a bargain; they had surrendered to White America a magnificent pastoral and mineral Nation, in return for six million acres they got a hundred square miles.

PURPOSE,

in the anterior, always followed methodically closely by the

ACTION

intended. We are such causal creatures locked into an ethics of intention—how else to level blame?

You can dream of creamy futures,
but actions have an urgency

all their own, the need to do it now.

The Navajo laughed.
No ordinary guilt pursued by ghosts
that might be driven off

singing, shaking rattles, by arrangements \
on the ground of magic stones,
bird claws, antelope hoofs,

but ADJUSTMENTS

to an irresistible flow.

ENTER

a bearded man, himself a cool marauder
who had torn and burned his way from
Atlanta to Savannah,

SHERMAN

came to Bosque Redondo.

A system now of forms and signatures, allotments of specific land, materials to build a house, revenues for a few tools, groceries, and a truck.

...it was as if a cloud had rolled back.

No more predations (as our Government had termed it) nor mornings in front of the Hogan, the sun coming up, the shadows painting canyon walls, the ponies pawing in the dust, ready to raid!

Never free inside a circle drawn by another's hand, being so circumscribed and touched on every surface,

LIMITED, diminished,

to unfree! Repeat, NOT free!

It was as if a cloud had rolled,
the darkness came in over them,
the moving darkness drawing a wall.

Each desire runs along the nerves
to the end, the shortened end
lines drawn forever on a map
etched with a sharp stone
drawn roughly.

Naabeehó Bináhásdzo
(Navajo Nation)

But the tribes of Indians inhabiting this country were fierce savages, whose occupation was war, and whose subsistence was drawn chiefly from the forest. To leave them in possession of their country, was to leave the country a wilderness; to govern them as a distinct people, was impossible, because they were as brave and as high spirited as they were fierce and were ready to repel by arms every attempt on their independence. **— John Marshall, Johnson and Graham's Lessee v. William McIntosh, 21 U.S. 543 (1823)**

1
Go back to your memories
of warriors, of peaches and roses,
and keep on dreaming how
you were going, one day,
to renew the old ways,
bring everything back, reborn,
new, but old, and lift up the Navajo!
How your leaders assured they would
someday lift you off the reservation,

Out of your poverty and disease, out of alcoholism and crime, violence and abuse.

That's dead, for more than now,
lost in the thick exhaust of old
motors, dirt floors, the blood wasted,

and the DISAPPOINTMENT.

And the fact is you're really

STUCK here

in the *Bilagáana*'s game, between
resignation and resistance.

DREAM *this:*

what if you could shed
the painted devils
hooked into your back?
What if you dreamed *Dinétah,*

as if no European had
ever crossed the Atlantic,
or ever anchored
in an American bay,
or dared touch the sacred soil
of *Mikinoc Waajew,* "Turtle Island?"

What if you dreamed North America
without White Americans!
A miracle of a new people, or better,
an old people made over young
in a dream,

CONJURING

virginal deserts, prairies, forests, rivers,
mountains, lakes, undulating grassy hills,
wild rocky coastlines, the sun forever
in its crossing, the clouds like Alps.

A bridge of dreams that has been
suspended, reaching over time and rocky
substance dragging the past
over, through, above, and despite
the present now, into a righteous future,

NAHASDZIAN, the day as mother.

Where the sky always comes up

BRIGHT white (*ligai*)

in the EAST

unannounced, from

the DARK black (*lizhin*),

turns to yellow (*litzo*)
with the sun, and the sky stretches,
imagining an ideal blue (*dootlizh*),
the blue of *lapis lazuli.*

Then *hogans* will all awake to the new world, still the old world—

Naabeehó Bináhásdzo! Diné Bikéyah! ahu! ahu!

What if Columbus had only dawdled
in Spain, fallen in love, and left
all the gold pesetas
in Isabella's treasury. And if
from New England to the Carolinas,
from the tip of Florida to

Guanahani in the Bahamas,
not a European would be found?

                    2
A Navajo boy, his wild daydreams
making an ancient ritual desert
Camelot, a chimera of warriors
the treasured

CORN,

of mountains to converse and visions;
this boy, who dares venture
into the wilderness alone,
in search of rumored ecstasy,
if only for a moment's ecstasy.

The time of their beginning is not told, they are coeval with the universe, and they still live-in distant lands, but not in the nether world where dead Navajos go; in short, they are immortal and eternal—they are gods. — **W.W. Matthews,** *American Naturalist (1886)*

Like a windblown bolt of vivid cloth, striped in the colors of the rainbow, the morning unfurls from all the points of the compass, distant mountains stand arrayed, and the mysterious *Sháńdíín* sets fire to the sand in the wind.

The town lights of Window Rock,
Tséghahoodzání
serially switch off in the increasing sun,
and long shadows stretch across
the Creek and on the rock walls
and sandstone wind-sculptures,
dark canyons at the bottom of the sea.

To voices now that no one hears
except the boy, singing voices,
echoes of the dance,
as if some Bedouin were
intoning desert songs,
the music resounding
off the red stone corridors.

He is ready, this boy, truly ready
to go back or go ahead. For him,
the Navajo, his people, are as purely
native to the earth as the beans,
the corn, the planted squash,
as the wild pale cottonwood
shoots in the river's bank.

He chants his memorized incantations.

Hózhó náhásdlíí'- Hózhó náhásdlíí'- Hózhó náhásdlíí'

3

Navajo society can incorporate the naachid and the role of the naataanii along with creativity to form a government that produces harmonious cooperation, coexistence founded on respect for autonomy, and the principle of self-determination. For example, in historical Diné society, leaders governed by Hozho, a relational principle that describes life as interconnected, balanced, and harmonious. It is a natural order of life. In Diné, it is known as hozhooji k'e iina (a Blessing Way of living life in relation to all living being. — **Lloyd L. Lee**

First of all, say again!

NO POTATOES OR CORN

in Europe. The dumb pull of this

FACT

forces a choice and scholars come to measure distances past that exact point of Time; what was and was to go no farther, and we can

DREAM

what will be, could be, would have been, and close our eyes.
Think how darkly sunned by the desert heat the Navajo, dark as the burned burl of *olneya tesota*, Ironwood, is darkened and hardened.

Time comes along swinging a bucket, the Future inhales the Past.
What do Merriam's Shrew and the Black-tailed Jackrabbit KNOW of Time?
We jump over them, Times's shards are whatever in the poem you think they are...hours, days, months, years, decades, centuries.

Dream a Navajo ambassador sent to *parlez* Susquehanna on matters of trade and Powhatan tourists, breathe on the magical corn pollen, baked on a mother-of-pearl plate from California's Abalone.
To make the best world
from dust, dream past it,
make

FOURS

of place, color, compass, mountains,
and the named winds,

IMAGINE hard enough

the WAY

standing on the stones to survey,

the BILAGAÁNA gone!

Gone!

We have words to summon up
an elastic past, to stretch it
over the present, to the future
words and worlds, just how a look
crosses mountains, skies, and valleys,

SEEING
with the mind's eye as if there'd never been

WHITES.
Weaving fancy and recall on an agile loom, dream whatever you can imagine, remember and transcend.

Trust now little things,
things unchanged no matter,
see yourselves reflected
in the mica surface on a tiny
stone lifted from the river.

*The female intellect. Women's intellect is manifested as perfect control, presence of mind, and utilization of all advantages. They bequeath it as their fundamental character to their children, and the father furnishes the darker background of will. His influence determines the rhythm and harmony, so to speak, to which the new life is to be played out; but its melody comes from the woman. — **Nietzsche***

Changing Woman (*Asdzą́ą́' Nádleehéi*) grows old or young, as necessary. She must be the present god-head, she holds the key. Born to be imagined leading the Navajo past the obstacle of Time, grown old and weakened then,

   but NOW,

   younger as when the warriors ranged the desert,
   when the peaches in Canyon de Chelly,
   hung heavy with peach juice,
   and the desert roses bloomed
   She will lead the *Diné* through the impassable

   GATES

   of Time.

Author Profile

Charles D. Tarlton

The author is a retired politics professor from California and New York who grew up in the Southwest enamored of the sights and scents of the desert, who has always been sad that he missed the heyday of the frontier. Poetry has always been central in his life, even as he pursued a career and a living teaching political ideas. In recent years he has focused almost entirely on writing poems, however, giving him the opportunity to compile a second résumé.

He lives on the shore, now, in Connecticut, with his wife, Ann Knickerbocker, an abstract painter, and Nikki, their black standard poodle.

www.ingramcontent.com/pod-product-compliance
Lightning Source LLC
Chambersburg PA
CBHW062146100526
44589CB00014B/1703